All kinds of Fish

WRITTEN BY **ANNE W. PHILLIPS** • ILLUSTRATED BY **JEAN PIDGEON**

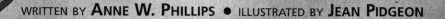

HARCOURT BRACE & COMPANY

Orlando   Atlanta   Austin   Boston   San Francisco   Chicago   Dallas   New York
Toronto   London

Fish with spots.
Fish with dots.

2

Fish with lines.
Fish with spines.

3

Fish with lumps.
Fish with bumps.

4

Fish with zigs.
Fish with zags.

Fish with stripes.
Yipes!

6

Fish with a fin.
Fish with a grin.

Swim, fish, swim!

8